SOME MAJOR EVENTS IN WORLD WAR II

THE EUROPEAN THEATER

1939 SEPTEMBER—Germany invades Poland; Great Britain, France, Australia, & New Zealand declare war on Germany; Battle of the Atlantic begins. NOVEMBER—Russia invades Finland.

1940 APRIL—Germany invades Denmark & Norway. MAY—Germany invades Belgium, Luxembourg, & The Netherlands; British forces retreat to Dunkirk and escape to England. JUNE—Italy declares war on Britain & France; France surrenders to Germany. JULY—Battle of Britain begins. SEPTEMBER—Italy invades Egypt; Germany, Italy, & Japan form the Axis countries. OCTOBER—Italy invades Greece. NOVEMBER—Battle of Britain over. DECEMBER—Britain attacks Italy in North Africa.

1941 JANUARY—Allies take Tobruk. FEBRUARY—Rommel arrives at Tripoli. APRIL—Germany invades Greece & Yugoslavia. JUNE—Allies are in Syria; Germany invades Russia. JULY—Russia joins Allies. AUGUST—Germans capture Kiev. OCTOBER—Germany reaches Moscow. DECEMBER—Germans retreat from Moscow; Japan attacks Pearl Harbor; United States enters war against Axis nations.

1942 MAY—first British bomber attack on Cologne. JUNE—Germans take Tobruk. SEPTEMBER—Battle of Stalingrad begins. OCTOBER—Battle of El Alamein begins. NOVEMBER—Allies recapture Tobruk; Russians counterattack at Stalingrad.

1943 JANUARY—Allies take Tripoli. FEBRUARY—German troops at Stalingrad surrender. APRIL—revolt of Warsaw Ghetto Jews begins. MAY—German and Italian resistance in North Africa is over; their troops surrender in Tunisia; Warsaw Ghetto revolt is put down by Germany. JULY—allies invade Sicily; Mussolini put in prison. SEPTEMBER—Allies land in Italy; Italians surrender; Germans occupy Rome; Mussolini rescued by Germany. OCTOBER—Allies capture Naples; Italy declares war on Germany. NOVEMBER—Russians recapture Kiev.

1944 JANUARY—Allies land at Anzio. JUNE—Rome falls to Allies; Allies land in Normandy (D-Day). JULY—assassination attempt on Hitler fails. AUGUST—Allies land in southern France. SEPTEMBER—Brussels freed. OCTOBER—Athens liberated. DECEMBER—Battle of the Bulge.

1945 JANUARY—Russians free Warsaw. FEBRUARY—Dresden bombed. APRIL—Americans take Belsen and Buchenwald concentration camps; Russians free Vienna; Russians take over Berlin; Mussolini killed; Hitler commits suicide. MAY—Germany surrenders; Goering captured.

THE PACIFIC THEATER

1940 SEPTEMBER—Japan joins Axis nations Germany & Italy.

1941 APRIL—Russia & Japan sign neutrality pact. DECEMBER—Japanese launch attacks against Pearl Harbor, Hong Kong, the Philippines, & Malaya; United States and Allied nations declare war on Japan; China declares war on Japan, Germany, & Italy; Japan takes over Guam, Wake Island, & Hong Kong; Japan attacks Burma.

1942 JANUARY—Japan takes over Manila; Japan invades Dutch East Indies. FEBRUARY—Japan takes over Singapore; Battle of the Java Sea. APRIL—Japanese overrun Bataan. MAY—Japan takes Mandalay; Allied forces in Philippines surrender to Japan; Japan takes Corregidor; Battle of the Coral Sea. JUNE—Battle of Midway; Japan occupies Aleutian Islands. AUGUST—United States invades Guadalcanal in the Solomon Islands.

1943 FEBRUARY—Guadalcanal taken by U.S. Marines. MARCH—Japanese begin to retreat in China. APRIL—Yamamoto shot down by U.S. Air Force. MAY—U.S. troops take Aleutian Islands back from Japan. JUNE—Allied troops land in New Guinea. NOVEMBER—U.S. Marines invade Bougainville & Tarawa.

1944 FEBRUARY—Truk liberated. JUNE—Saipan attacked by United States. JULY—battle for Guam begins. OCTOBER—U.S. troops invade Philippines; Battle of Leyte Gulf won by Allies.

1945 JANUARY—Luzon taken; Burma Road won back. MARCH—Iwo Jima freed. APRIL—Okinawa attacked by U.S. troops; President Franklin Roosevelt dies; Harry S. Truman becomes president. JUNE—United States takes Okinawa. AUGUST—atomic bomb dropped on Hiroshima; Russia declares war on Japan; atomic bomb dropped on Nagasaki. SEPTEMBER—Japan surrenders.

WORLD AT WAR

Battle of
Leyte Gulf

WORLD AT WAR

Battle of Leyte Gulf

By G.C. Skipper

 CHILDRENS PRESS, CHICAGO

On December 7, 1941, the Japanese bombed Pearl Harbor (above).
Within eight months, they controlled much of the Central
Pacific Ocean.

FRONTISPIECE:

A suicide hit by a Japanese plane created
fires and explosions on the American ship
Suwanee during the Battle of Leyte Gulf.

Library of Congress Cataloging in Publication Data

Skipper, G.C.
  The battle of Leyte Gulf.

  (His World at war)
  SUMMARY: Details the October, 1944 battle between
the Japanese and the Americans in which the Japanese
fighting navy was virtually destroyed.
  1. Philippine Sea, Battles of the, 1944—Juvenile
literature. [1. Philippine Sea, Battles of the, 1944.
2. World War, 1939-1945—Pacific Ocean] I. Title.
II. Series.
D774.P5S58   940.54'26   80-27265
ISBN 0-516-04788-4

PICTURE CREDITS:

NATIONAL ARCHIVES: Cover, pages 4, 9
(bottom), 21, 22, 26, 29, 30, 36, 37, 38, 41,
43, 45, 46

OFFICIAL U.S. NAVY PHOTOGRAPH: pages 6,
13, 17, 18

UPI: pages 9 (top), 25, 31, 33, 40

LEN MEENTS (maps): pages 10, 14, 35

COVER PHOTO:

Crewman fight fires on the *Princeton* after
an explosion following a Japanese dive-
bomber attack during the Battle of Leyte
Gulf.

By August of 1942, only eight months had passed since the Japanese had bombed Pearl Harbor. But already they controlled important island groups in the Central Pacific Ocean. These included the Carolines, Marianas, Marshalls, and Gilberts. The Japanese used many of these islands as air bases. Japan had also occupied the Philippine Islands since January of 1942.

Between November of 1943 and August of 1944, Allied troops took several of these islands from the Japanese. Tarawa and Makin in the Gilbert Islands were taken in November, 1943. Kwajalein, Majoro, and Eniwetok in the Marshalls were occupied in January and February of 1944. Saipan, Guam, and Tinian in the Marianas were taken in July and August.

From their new air bases in the Marianas, the Allies were close enough to attack both Japan and the Philippines by air. In September of 1944, marines and army troops invaded Peleliu, in the Palau Islands. They also took Morotai, in the

Netherlands East Indies. Occupation of these islands brought the Allies even closer to the Philippines—close enough for naval forces to attack. They intended to retake these islands from the Japanese.

On October 20, 1944, Allied forces landed on Leyte Island in the central Philippines. The Japanese were not about to let them stay. They planned to have their navy drive the Allies out. They intended to destroy the hundreds of American ships that were anchored in Leyte Gulf.

Vice Admiral Takeo Kurita was the commander of the First Strike Force. It was one of the Japanese fleets that would be a part of this battle. His ships had set sail from the southern coast of Borneo on October 22, 1944. Now, at dawn on the 23rd, the fleet was ploughing through the water toward its target—the United States ships massed at Leyte.

On October 20, 1944, Allied forces landed on Leyte Island in the central Philippines. From here, they intended to take the rest of the Philippine Islands from the Japanese.

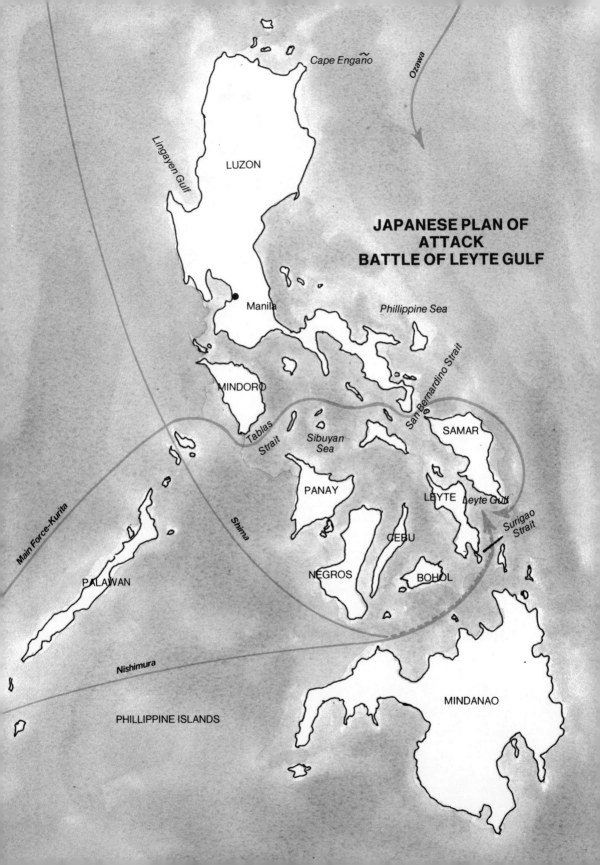

Kurita was not happy with his attack orders. There was too much risk involved. Even now his fleet was nearing a stretch of uncharted water west of Palawan Island. This area was called the Dangerous Ground. Kurita thought they just might be able to move through these waters without being attacked by the Americans. But he would still have to take the fleet through San Bernardino Strait. Then he would have to turn south past Samar Island and enter Leyte Gulf from the east. That was a lot of open water. Nevertheless, Kurita planned to follow his orders precisely.

Kurita thought about the Second Strike Force. It was commanded by Vice Admiral Shoji Nishimura. Nishimura's ships were supposed to enter Leyte Gulf from the south, making their way through Surigao Strait. Kurita shook his head. He gazed out over the water. Surigao Strait lay between Mindanao and Leyte. It was very narrow. And it could be very dangerous.

If the timing were right and there was no interference, the two strike forces would meet in Leyte Gulf. They would then be in a position to wipe out the Americans.

It was probably a good plan, Kurita told himself. If it worked, it would give Japan hope for victory in World War II. But there were still too many risks.

The First Strike Force steamed nearer to the Dangerous Ground. Suddenly a tremendous explosion ripped through the stillness of the sea. Kurita knew immediately that the fleet had been spotted by the Americans. They were being attacked!

The sudden gunfire and explosions were deafening. Kurita was watching two of his cruisers, the *Maya* and the *Takao*. Suddenly they both jerked and leaped like wild horses. The *Maya* began to sink.

Vice Admiral Takeo Kurita, the commander of the First Strike Force

Men were yelling all around him. His own ship, the *Atago*, lurched to one side. Fire erupted across the deck.

"We've been hit!" someone yelled.

Another ship in the First Strike Force lurched. American firepower from two submarines, the *Darter* and the *Dace*, had cut loose on the Japanese fleet.

The Japanese increased their speed. Their engines were powerful. Soon they had outrun the two United States submarines.

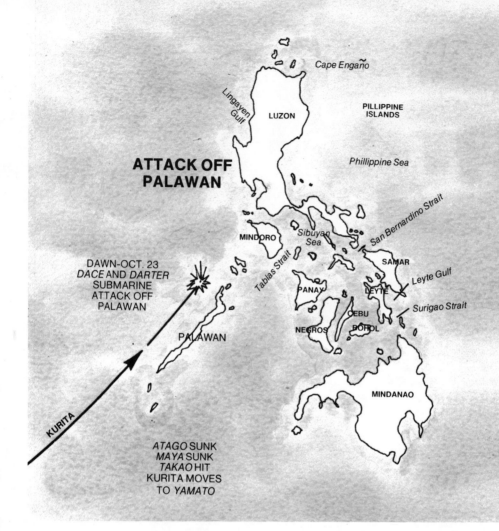

ATTACK OFF
PALAWAN

Cape Engaño

PILLIPPINE
ISLANDS

Lingayen Gulf

LUZON

Phillippine Sea

San Bernardino Strait

MINDORO

Sibuyan Sea

DAWN–OCT. 23
DACE AND *DARTER*
SUBMARINE
ATTACK OFF
PALAWAN

Tablas Strait

SAMAR

Leyte Gulf

PANAY

LEYTE

Surigao Strait

PALAWAN

CEBU

NEGROS

BOHOL

KURITA

MINDANAO

ATAGO SUNK
MAYA SUNK
TAKAO HIT
KURITA MOVES
TO *YAMATO*

"Get the admiral to another ship. Hurry!"
someone yelled. The flagship *Atago* was sinking.
However, Kurita and his staff were quickly
transferred to a larger ship, the *Yamato*. This ship
was to be Kurita's command ship for the rest of
the voyage. It was a huge, ultramodern battleship
equipped with enormous guns.

In the same fleet was the *Yamato*'s sister ship, the *Musashi*. The *Musashi* was even more up-to-date than the *Yamato*. It was a super battleship, a giant. And it was equipped with huge, powerful guns that had never before been fired. The *Musashi* had a pagodalike structure reaching high into the sky.

Aboard the *Yamato*, Kurita reviewed his orders. He was very worried. The fleet had not even reached the waters of the Central Philippines and already two of his cruisers had been sunk. Another, the *Takao*, was so badly damaged that she had to turn back for Borneo.

Kurita's fleet was traveling in two circular formations. These two groups were seven miles apart. In the center of the first circle were the *Yamato* and the *Musashi*. In the center of the second circle was the *Kongo*. They steamed ahead toward San Bernardino Strait. There they would break through to Leyte Gulf.

Kurita thought about his superior officer, Admiral Soemu Toyoda. Toyoda was the commander-in-chief of the Combined Fleet. He had come up with a plan to make sure that the Leyte Gulf attack would succeed. At the moment, United States Admiral William F. (Bull) Halsey's Third Fleet was in the way of a Japanese attack. His ships were strung out across the Philippine Sea from mid-Luzon to Leyte. Halsey would have to be pulled away from San Bernardino Strait. Then Kurita's ships would be able to get through safely.

Toyoda had sent Vice Admiral Jisaburo Ozawa, the supreme commander, on a decoy mission. Ozawa's fleet was even now steaming toward Halsey's Third Fleet. Ozawa was coming from the north. He was to bring his ships south along the eastern shore of Luzon. Ozawa's force looked strong. His fleet appeared to be the main striking force. Actually, there were very few aircraft and pilots in this fleet. They wouldn't be able to do

Vice Admiral Jisaburo Ozawa, the supreme commander, was in charge of the decoy force coming from the north.

much damage. That didn't matter to the Japanese. As long as Halsey believed this was the main strike force, their goal would be achieved.

Toyoda wanted Ozawa to force the Third Fleet to chase him. If Halsey took the bait, the Third Fleet would head north toward Ozawa's fleet. San Bernardino Strait would be unprotected. Kurita would then be able to get through the strait. Kurita hoped Toyoda's plan would work.

Vice Admiral Shoji Nishimura (left) and Vice Admiral Kiyohide Shima (right) planned to enter Leyte Gulf from the south, making their way through Surigao Strait.

And what about Nishimura? Kurita hoped he had not run into any trouble. And no telling what Shima's fleet of ships was doing. Vice Admiral Kiyohide Shima had a very small force. Shima had not even been included in the original attack plans. Yet he had been given permission to join in the Leyte Gulf battle. At last word, Shima was trailing along behind Nishimura. Maybe both of them will have better luck than we've had, Kurita thought now.

Kurita's force, moving in its circular formation, was nearing the Sibuyan Sea. It was dawn on October 24. So far, all had been quiet.

"We've located the enemy fleet again, sir," an officer told Admiral Halsey. "It's off Mindoro Island."

"Good," Halsey replied. He promptly ordered an attack. Later that morning, the aircraft from Halsey's Third Fleet carriers found Kurita's ships. The roaring drone of their engines seemed to fill the entire sky. Kurita looked upward. He squinted against the sun. American torpedo planes and bombers were everywhere!

Kurita shouted an order. At once, the antiaircraft guns aboard his ships pointed skyward. They zeroed in on the Americans and opened fire.

Kurita knew his ships could throw more tons of shells than anything else afloat. He felt confident that his guns would wipe out the American planes.

The antiaircraft guns barked and recoiled. Huge tongues of flame shot skyward. The flames paled in the midday sun. The shells shot upward toward the American planes.

The noise was earsplitting. The guns roared and jumped, one after another. Kurita watched anxiously from the deck of the *Yamato*. He was looking for the sudden trail of smoke that would signal the death of an American plane.

No such signal came. The planes kept coming. Somehow, they made their way through the enormous barrage of gunfire from Kurita's ships. Suddenly a group of American planes emerged from the dense smoke thrown up by the guns. They were headed straight for the *Yamato*! No, Kurita realized. They were after the *Musashi*!

The planes swarmed down. They fired their machine guns. They released their torpedoes and bombs. Water flew upward all around the Japanese ships. Some of the ships were damaged.

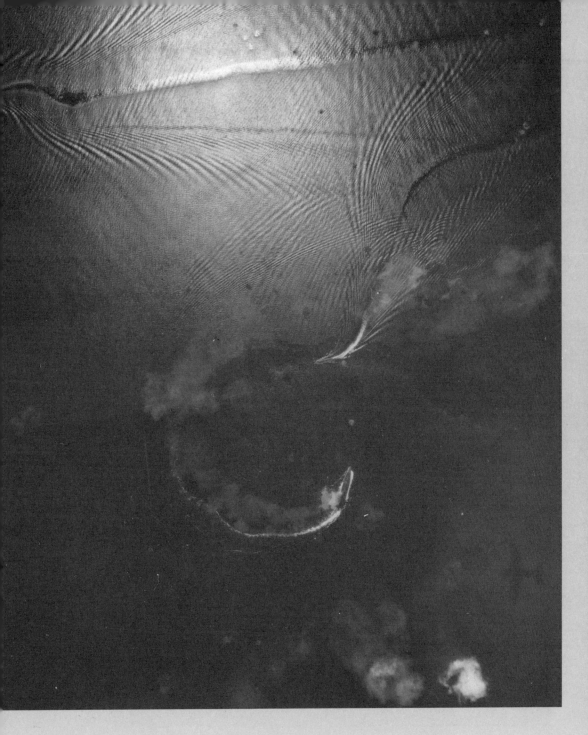

Japanese ships circle and swerve to avoid aerial attacks by United States Navy planes at Tablas Strait. During this attack, the huge Japanese battleship *Musashi* was crippled.

Japanese warships in the Sibuyan Sea under attack by United States Navy bombers.

But so far there had been no direct hits. The two super battleships kept right on steaming toward San Bernardino Strait.

Then there was another attack. The *Musashi,* already suffering from an earlier hit, was hit again. "The Palace," as the great ship was called, shook and shivered. She had been hit by three torpedoes. Still she kept moving.

Kurita, aboard the *Yamato,* was stunned. He was thankful that his own ship had not been hit. He watched the *Yamato*'s sister ship. He felt that truly these were ships that could not be sunk. Certainly not by these enemy planes.

As Kurita saw the aircraft swarming down again and again, he knew something had to be done. His fleet wouldn't be able to hold off the American aircraft forever.

Kurita sent an urgent message for help: "We are being subjected to repeated enemy carrier-based air attacks. Advise immediately of contacts and attacks made by you on the enemy."

Kurita handed the message to an aide. "Send this to Manila and Ozawa! Hurry!"

Kurita continued to watch the battle rage around him. Then, though it didn't seem possible, things got much worse. Fifteen minutes after Kurita had radioed for help, the Americans launched another assault. This time, twenty-nine planes dove directly down on the *Musashi*. The entire sky seemed filled with Americans.

Four bombs, one right after the other, smashed into the *Musashi*. Suddenly a torpedo hit her hull. The giant battleship lurched. She was badly damaged. Her speed dropped. She fell behind the *Yamato*.

"Reduce speed!" Kurita commanded. "We must slow down so the *Musashi* can keep up!"

Suddenly Kurita realized that he wouldn't be able to get to Leyte Gulf in time to meet Nishimura. Not at this slower speed. He would be late in joining in the attack. He had to have help *now*. Kurita sent out another urgent message.

Navy bomber scores a hit on a Japanese light carrier.
This picture was taken from the attacking plane.

There was still one more way out of the trouble,
Kurita realized. The giant guns aboard the
crippled *Musashi* had never been fired. They were
being saved for the battle at Leyte. If the guns
were as powerful as they were supposed to be, they
could blast the American aircraft out of the air.

As Kurita watched, he realized that the
commander aboard the *Musashi* had had the same
thought. The big guns suddenly pointed toward
the sky.

The American planes remained untouched by the Japanese counterattack and continued their own attack on Kurita's ships.

There was great excitement on the *Musashi*. The big guns were going into action!

The guns bellowed. They were so powerful that the giant battleship, big as it was, was shoved backward by the recoil. It looked as if she had been hit by another torpedo. Her guns continued to send the huge shells skyward. The big ship lunged backward with each blast.

But not one single American plane was hit. Untouched, they all continued to attack.

Three more torpedoes swished across the water. They smashed into the *Musashi.* Then a bomb screamed down. It exploded on the deck. Then seven more torpedoes found their mark. They tore into the huge ship.

Suddenly the American planes turned and were gone. Kurita's First Strike Force was stunned. Still, the ships steamed ahead. They had to reach San Bernardino Strait.

At about three-thirty that afternoon, however, the Americans came back. They were determined to sink the *Musashi.* The ship was ordered to return to Borneo immediately.

The *Musashi* fell back and turned. She headed back to safety as ordered. But she was suffering from seventeen bomb hits and nineteen torpedo hits. She never made it to home port. She sank that evening. Half her crew went down with her.

Because he was chasing Ozawa, Halsey left the San Bernardino Strait unprotected. There were no large American ships there to stop Kurita.

Kurita sensed that the situation had improved. He reversed his course again. He started back toward San Bernardino Strait. He grew closer and closer. Still no enemy planes came after him. Kurita could hardly believe his good luck. He decided to send a message to Nishimura. He would be late getting to Leyte Gulf. Nishimura, however, should go ahead with the attack plans. Kurita would get there as soon as he could.

Meanwhile, Kurita continued to steam toward San Bernardino Strait. He had made up his mind to get to Leyte Gulf. Nothing would stand in his way.

The late afternoon sun sank lower in the sky. Kurita had the uneasy feeling that the Americans were not finished. The thought of more enemy planes swarming down on him was on his mind during the entire afternoon.

At four o'clock Kurita made a decision. He would not push his fleet onward. He was sure the Americans were planning another attack. He did

This wounded pilot has just returned to his carrier "home," the *Lexington*, after taking part in the aerial attack on Kurita's First Strike Force in the Sibuyan Sea.

not want his fleet to be caught in the narrow San Bernardino Strait in daylight.

"Reverse course!" he commanded.

The mighty battleships began to turn slowly. Gradually they changed direction. Soon they were steaming west. Kurita watched the sun sinking lower and lower. At every moment he expected the Americans to return. But they didn't appear. Kurita steamed west for an hour. Still no American planes came after him.

Admiral William F. (Bull) Halsey, commanding officer of the Third Fleet.

Kurita was puzzled. He didn't know what to make of the quiet. Didn't the Americans have sense enough to take advantage of the daylight? Why didn't they strike while they could?

What Kurita did not know at the time was that the decoy had worked. Ozawa's ships had attracted the attention of Admiral Halsey. Halsey was sure he had spotted the main Japanese striking force. Just before dawn on October 25, Halsey took off after Ozawa with everything he had.

Vice Admiral Thomas C. Kinkaid (left) was ready when Nishimura's Second Strike Force entered Surigao Strait.

Meanwhile, Nishimura had made progress. He had run into no enemy aircraft or ships. Untouched, he reached the Surigao Strait at 11:00 P.M. the night of October 24. He didn't know that the Americans, under Vice Admiral Thomas C. Kinkaid, knew he was coming. They were lying in wait in Surigao Strait. Nishimura's luck had run out. Almost as soon as he entered the strait, he was attacked by torpedoes from PT boats. Guns roared from old battleships and cruisers.

The Japanese fought back. But the Americans continued firing. They knocked Nishimura's fleet with a solid punch. When the Americans pulled back to regroup, many of Nishimura's ships were badly damaged.

Still the commander of the Second Strike Force kept going. He was close to his target—nearly through Surigao Strait, nearly to Leyte Gulf itself. He wasn't about to stop now.

The Americans came back in a second assault. They hit hard. Nishimura had finally entered Leyte Gulf. But he was still a long way from his target. Why didn't Kurita arrive? If he would only show up with his fleet!

Even as Nishimura thought of help, his own ship was struck. The mighty flagship *Yamashiro* lurched in the water. The Americans had been right on target. The ship held up as long as it could. Finally, at 4:19 A.M., October 25, the *Yamashiro* gave a mighty sigh and sank. Nishimura and most of the crew died with the ship.

One of the Japanese ships that didn't quite make it to Leyte Gulf sank in Surigao Strait after this direct hit by a Navy Curtiss Hellcat.

While the battle with Nishimura was in full swing, Shima kept his steady pace. He had been about thirty miles behind Nishimura. At 4:20 A.M., only moments after Nishimura's ship had sunk, Shima blundered into the battle area.

All around him Shima could see signs of the battle. Dead ships were all over the water. Some were burning out of control. Ahead of him, Shima saw two ships burning. As he drew closer, he realized it was only one ship. One of the great battleships had been split in two! Both sections were burning in the water.

Too late Shima realized that Nishimura had run into real trouble. But before he could leave the area, he was attacked by American PT boats.

Suddenly Shima went pale. One of Nishimura's surviving ships was heading full speed toward Shima's fleet! It was trying to escape. As Shima watched, the ships *Nachi* and *Mogami* slammed together. As they collided in the water, Shima whirled away from the railing of his ship. "Turn around!" he shouted. "Get out of here! We're too late to help!"

As Shima's fleet made its turn, more United States PT boats came in to attack. Then, at dawn, aircraft from the Seventh Fleet joined the attack. Shima's fleet was destroyed very quickly. Sudden quiet fell across Leyte Gulf.

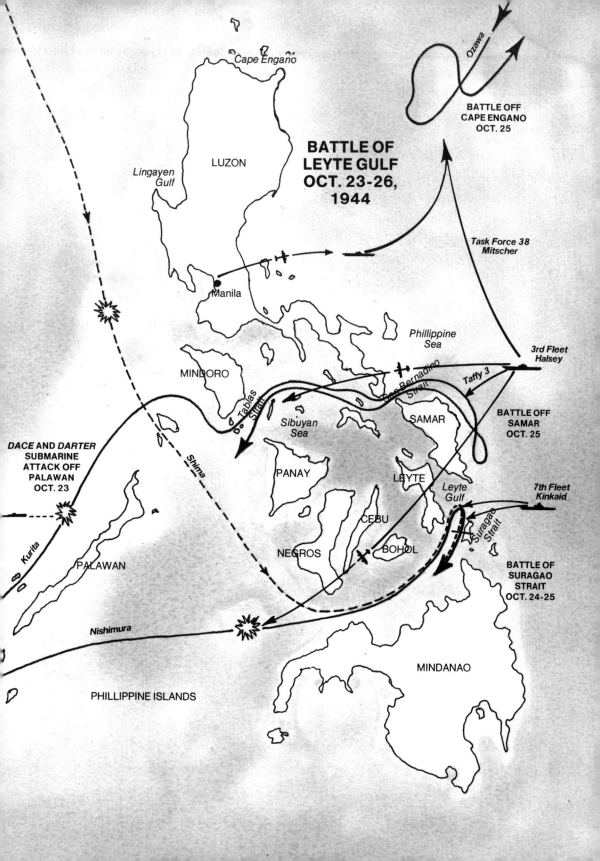

Cape Engaño

LUZON

Lingayen
Gulf

**BATTLE OF
LEYTE GULF
OCT. 23-26,
1944**

Ozawa

**BATTLE OFF
CAPE ENGAÑO
OCT. 25**

*Task Force 38
Mitscher*

Manila

*Phillippine
Sea*

*3rd Fleet
Halsey*

MINDORO

San Bernadino Strait

Taffy 3

**DACE AND DARTER
SUBMARINE
ATTACK OFF
PALAWAN
OCT. 23**

Tablas Strait

*Sibuyan
Sea*

SAMAR

**BATTLE OFF
SAMAR
OCT. 25**

Shima

PANAY

LEYTE

*Leyte
Gulf*

*7th Fleet
Kinkaid*

Kurita

CEBU

Suragao Strait

PALAWAN

NEGROS

BOHOL

**BATTLE OF
SURAGAO
STRAIT
OCT. 24-25**

Nishimura

MINDANAO

PHILLIPPINE ISLANDS

On these pages: While Nishimura's and Shima's ships were being
attacked by Kinkaid's forces in Surigao Strait, Halsey's Third
Fleet forces were doing battle with Ozawa's decoy force
in the north, off Cape Engaño.

Men aboard the carrier Essex (above) fire antiaircraft guns at attacking
Japanese planes during the battle.

A Japanese plane comes down in a suicide dive on the carrier *Lexington* (above). The plane struck the ship, causing an explosion. (The newly built aircraft carrier *Lexington* had been given the same name as the carrier that went down during the Battle of the Coral Sea.)

The Japanese aircraft carriers *Zuikaku* and *Shokaku* (above) are under attack by Halsey's forces off Cape Engaño. Another Japanese carrier, the *Zuiho* (below) is about to be hit by a torpedo. This very low aerial picture was taken from the plane that fired the torpedo. The *Zuiho* sank shortly afterward.

The morning of October 25 had dawned overcast and dreary. The ocean was choppy. Kurita's ships bounced and dipped as they moved through San Bernardino Strait. Kurita expected the Americans to attack at any time. No attack came. The ships moved right on through the strait. They slipped into the Philippine Sea.

Kurita breathed a sigh of relief. He gave an order. It was 6:27 A.M. Kurita's ships, following his command, formed a circle around the *Yamato*. The ships moved forward. They were now off Samar Island.

Suddenly, Kurita saw a group of carriers and destroyers. He thought it must be the main American striking force. He didn't know it was only the cover force for the American landings at Leyte—a task group called Taffy 3. Kurita's guns began firing immediately.

The men of Taffy 3 had been taken by surprise off Samar Island. This crewman aboard one of the American aircraft carriers makes a dash across the deck as Kurita's force attacks.

The Americans had been taken by surprise. They didn't have time to react in strength. It took them awhile to rearm their planes and send them up from the carrier decks. The Americans had been so sure that Ozawa's fleet, now being chased by Halsey, was the main Japanese force.

But here they were. The battle was on. And all Taffy 3 had to fight with were a small group of escort carriers and destroyers. They knew they wouldn't last long against the powerful guns and antiaircraft weapons Kurita had. Still they fought. They got their planes in the air and attacked again and again.

"General attack!" Kurita ordered.

The Japanese ships broke formation. They went after the Americans any way they could.

A full-scale battle raged across the water. Kurita, in the midst of the battle, didn't realize that more United States ships were closing in behind his fleet.

Suddenly a squall came up. Sheets of rain poured down. No one could see anything through the downpour.

American crewman fight a fire on the *Princeton*. The fire was caused by an explosion following a Japanese dive-bomber attack,

This was the moment Taffy 3 had been waiting for. The planes pulled back into the clouds for a breather. Then they came out with guns blazing. They wanted to force the Japanese ships further out into the water. There another group of Americans, Taffy 2, was approaching.

The planes swept down on Kurita's ships. They attacked again and again. Slowly Kurita's ships were drawn further out. His fleet was face to face with the American ships. The battle blazed into full force. Despite the enormous size and power of the Japanese ships, the smaller American ships kept coming. They fired their guns. They launched their torpedoes. They sent up their planes. They fought furiously. They fought with more determination than Kurita had ever seen. But the Americans knew they would not be able to continue much longer. Help was far away, and Taffy 3 wasn't strong enough to hold on.

The American escort carriers *St. Lo* (above) and *Gambier Bay* (below) were two casualties of the Battle off Samar.

Then suddenly Kurita ordered his ships to withdraw. He was on the verge of a great victory. But he thought Halsey and Kinkaid were on the way with their fleets. He was afraid his fleet would be wiped out.

One by one the Japanese ships pulled back. They withdrew and steamed back to San Bernardino Strait. They moved on through the strait. There, Kurita ran into a hail of bullets from American planes. His ship, the *Yamato*, was badly damaged, but Kurita did not stop. He pushed his fleet further and further back from Leyte.

Kurita finally made it back to Borneo. He still did not know that he had backed away from victory.

When the Battle of Leyte Gulf was over, the Japanese fighting navy was just about finished. The United States had destroyed three Japanese

Lieutenant Commander Arthur L. Downing of the Third Fleet
scores a direct hit on Kurita's ship, the *Yamato*, in Surigao Strait.

battleships, including the two giant ships. They
had also destroyed four aircraft carriers, ten
cruisers, and nine destroyers. The Americans had
lost only three carriers and three destroyers.

Japan had lost an important battle. Never again
would the Japanese navy unite in a single, strong
fighting force.

And the United States had started the great
drive to take the Philippines.

PT boats patrol Leyte Gulf after the battle is over

INDEX

Page numbers in boldface type indicate illustrations

INDEX, Cont'd

About the Author

A native of Alabama, G.C. Skipper has traveled throughout the world, including Jamaica, Haiti, India, Argentina, the Bahamas, and Mexico. He has written several other children's books as well as an adult novel. Mr. Skipper has also published numerous articles in national magazines. He is now working on his second adult novel. Mr. Skipper and his family live in North Wales, Pennsylvania, a suburb of Philadelphia.